# THE HEIGHT IN BETWEEN

ALSO BY TIMOTHY HOUGHTON

High Bridges

Below Two Skies *(an Orchises book)*

Riding Untouched *(an Orchises book)*

Drop Light *(an Orchises book)*

# THE HEIGHT IN BETWEEN

TIMOTHY HOUGHTON

ORCHISES

WASHINGTON

2012

Copyright © 2012 Timothy Houghton

Library of Congress Cataloging Publication Data

Houghton, Timothy, 1955-
The height in between / Timothy Houghton.
p. cm.
ISBN 978-1-932535-26-6 (alk. paper)
I. Title.
PS3558.O848.H45 2012
811'.54—dc22
2011011779

Some of these poems (a few in earlier versions) appeared in the following journals: *Artlife*: "Empty Black Pages"; *Askew*: "Happy Tongue" and "Behind the Mobile of Planets"; *Delaware Poetry Review*: "Ice Elf," "The Healthy," and "Late Afternoon at Kolac's the Sun is Remade"; *Gargoyle*: "Homage to Sergio Leone"; *Mirror Northwest*: "The Neighbor's Truck" and "Silent Home Movie"; *New Mexico Poetry Review*: "Above It, Below It" and "Bull Snake"; *Poet Lore*: "A Chinese Mantis"; *SNReview*: "Road Cut"; *South Dakota Review*: "Redwoods: Northern California" and "To the Brown Recluse"; and *Stride Magazine*: "My Dolls."

"Bible Oil," "Birthday Party," "Modestly Alive," and "Mother Cartoon" appeared in *Chelsea*; "At the Artist Retreat," "Collector," "Emerson," "Ghost Bat," "Teaching," and "This Place Is Mine" were published in *Stand*.

I wish to express my gratitude to The Caldera Residency Program, The Hambidge Center, Hawthornden Castle International Retreat, The MacDowell Colony, and The Norton Island Residency Program for fellowships allowing me to work on these poems.

Special thanks to Dan Langton, Alfredo de Palchi, Derek Sheffield, Steve Snyder—and to Cindy Moore—for their support or advice as this book took shape.

ORCHISES PRESS
P. O. BOX 320533
ALEXANDRIA, VA 22320-4533

G 6 E 4 C 2 A

*for Roger Lathbury*

## Contents

*I*

Mother Cartoon     11
Birthday Party     13
Empty Black Pages     15
Bible Oil     16
Road Cut     18
Silent Home Movie     19
Behind the Mobile of Planets     20
Peace     22
Ice Elf     23


*II*

Effaced     27
Cozy Restaurant     28
Encounter     30
At the Artist Retreat     32
Fallen     33
Teaching     35
Collector     37
Modestly Alive     39
A Room for Last Rites     42
Above It, Below It     43
Wavelengths     44
Emerson     47
The Healthy     49

*III*

Redwoods: Northern California     53
Ghost Bat     56
Bull Snake     58
The Parrot Left Behind     60
A Chinese Mantis     64
Hooded Warbler     66
To the Brown Recluse     68


*IV*

This Place Is Mine     73
My Dolls     75
Homage to Sergio Leone     76
"Smooth Bore, Scattergun"     78
His Secret     80
The Neighbor's Truck     82
Italian Cook     84
Selective     86
Late Afternoon at Kolac's the Sun Is Remade     87
Happy Tongue     89
The Windmill Machine     91
Killing Art     93

# I

> *as when*
> *turning around, and, sweeping clear your forehead*
> *of its cloud of hair,*
>
> *you waved to me — and entered the dark.*
>
> — Eugenio Montale

## Mother Cartoon

Tenacious
with a troubled will,

she has perfected escape.

    She joins the mice and roaches surrounding the living room.

    She grabs a hole from her Acme kit,
    slaps it onto the wall,
    and jumps in

because we complain: the smell of mold,
dirt everywhere, ground into roots of the old shag—

in the bathroom,
a raccoon family peers from cracks in tile above the tub.

~

Our mother loves—she feeds the crafty rat in her mind
as Follain's man

fed a rat, to keep it from eating his books.
Twisted knots in the past
go unnamed

though I wonder what happens in the silence at night
and if the sound of the Boulevard creek

softens what comes to her.
Surely pain is here—

from secret rooms, from blows that have gone unfaced —
so that life is a burial.

~

The air's bad for breathing? Says who?

She leaves town fast when words catch up to her.
She takes straight lips into the hole and never explains.

> When she returns, we hear stories
> of lives in the dark, each one

the same as her own, well-lighted by her mind,
utterly normal.

## BIRTHDAY PARTY

The black metal door
caging the power

of the oil furnace
dropped down with a bang—

my dad picked each of us up
to see the flames

burst from newspaper wads
we threw into the pit. We laughed,

scared of its hunger
where it rumbled and waited

behind wooden screens
in a living-room nook

close to cake and candles, thrilled
when he pretended

to throw us in. The pressure
of heat blowing

from the hole—we thought explosion
like a TV bomb

from Colonel Savage's B-17.
We hoped it would happen,

we dove under furniture
in bliss.

        But that day's gone

like the memory,
on your hand,

of a dead pet.

        Now we're beaten up,
        nerves shot,

and it's quiet we want,
deliverance

from the smallest tensions
and fears:

        the relentless burnings
        of each candle.

## Empty Black Pages

Illness—
then he died.

Empty black pages
finish the album,

the way history
ended, too,

for my grandmother
who gave it to me

with a quick "Here,"
a stiff backbone

of anger,
her eyes distant

on the floor,
the reach of her arm

a vast scale
extending

her son to me.

# Bible Oil

*Revelation*

The boy knows how far to go
and squirms in the pew

below the threshold
of mom's eyes. The minister talks a red glow

in the curving arms of a stained-glass scene,
and the boy settles down    and takes his eyes down

to the black Bible in the slot before him. The ritual
begins—odd how that can happen,

how something unspeakable can ever quite begin.
Reaching for the book,

he touches the back of the bench,
the slick varnish on his fingers—then the cover,

its leather shine    like dirty oil on the garage floor
where he'd followed his father's work.

Years later, he knew it defined him,
the chaos of time    calmly operating

while earth's gravity holds it tight
like a collapsed ruin, a home of sorts. Now the boy

opens to Philippians, his fingers sliding down a thin page
that could tear in an instant—

an architecture of columns and tiny letters,
a maze of black branches in winter:

he sees crows, other inhabitants,
and comes to the words he's looking for: *the peace*

*which passeth understanding*
needed to fix the death of his father. Vague

imaginings     like blood vessels
give texture to the atmosphere—

a short joy
that stills him     that steels him. The rest is mere empire,

existence. Most of the time he's already old,
waiting for the words     *surely I come quickly*.

# Road Cut

*exposed by demolition*

Here's a design once pounded by winds,
its life taken by minerals —
a fern you'd find in any wet woods, except the skilled
rock that explains it.
        ~

        One Sunday he
pretended — too much hesitance,   too much effort
on display. He knew it was *the last time*
before I knew it, the smile on his face
both acted and felt,   the anxiety
a templet —
        the hospital room won't leave my mind
        (window, light, five people,
        the terrible matte texture
        of space itself),
a dwelling for many years — not every day,
just off and on   like long-wave peaks from a resting brain
hooked to an EEG.
        I've tried often to put myself in his place,
to understand his trial, his mind
with body stuck on a bed,
        trying to think
        beyond the limits
of empathy,   in order to carry him forward.

## Silent Home Movie

I don't believe it—
my birthday plain before me. Chunks of sky

hug balloons
tied floating

against the fretted dining room window. Punch,
ice cream, and kids—incredible

how much the brain abandons
in deference

to adulthood,
the genes of survival. I replay it, twice more,

wanting to remember
blowing out three candles,

but the lungs of those days no longer flourish in the brain.

Later, in the fatigue and darkness of night,
the pillow a soft watch

around my head. . .    I can't even pretend
to bring it back.

## Behind the Mobile of Planets

The baby growls,
dreams in territory

where animals practice
their lives.   I touch one cheek

then the other—each time
he turns away, content

with his own warmth.

~

Through a blank
far-away gaze

and lips shut tight,
he issues a hum

in monotone—
like the moon in its pale

morning form.

~

My face behind
the mobile of planets—

maybe that
will stay with him

vaguely, not quite thin as air:

a place to stretch the arms
with little resistance.

# Peace

*a crucifix*

Five years old,
he sucked a jawbreaker

down the wrong pipe. Jesus on the Cross
watched from the mantle.

Our mother
shouted *Jesus, oh Jesus*

and stuck a finger
into my brother's throat,

pushing the ball
farther down.

Ben was a wide-eyed robot,
frozen on his legs,

head tilted
a little to the side. I beat his back

with my fist
and the candy flew out,

marking the wall with purple. Later
our mom joked
    *—but it wasn't a joke—*

that Jesus raised his head
and bravely pointed a finger.

## Ice Elf

Where a foot-high *helper*
spent the night
sleeping—

        there's a compression and
        voice of mine

        partly buried in powder snow:

a quartz-like tower beside the wall
where pipe vents furnace.
                      One night my son
                        recreates it,

shaping air without precision
before the fireplace, but I see it,

the ice elf in his manic hands. He believes me
when I tell him
        *it doesn't leave tracks*
        *when the body runs away.*

His small hands are God, his talk behind them is God.
This immortality will live two more years,

maybe three. Yet I believe, too, angry
with innocence and angry at it.

~

I live in a family tightly packed
within a living room of worn furniture.

We watch TV at night. We sit in the air of light bulbs
and enjoy our smiles.

The hippie Christ adds dimension above the fireplace
with His soft beige shirt.

## II

*You don't want to hear the crows cry*
*The diminishing number of lines*
*To be spoken on this stage, set for how long*
*The shadow grows...*

—Claire Malroux

EFFACED

A young woman with sunglasses, black
bikini, blond hair

lies on a granite slab of shoreline
close to where I'm tapping
                         for tiny geysers,

digging into sand
to catch clams—

               she lies against stone
               like an inscription

designed for me: *Not
for you, 2010.*
               Oh, I think, she'd come

to enjoy
my patience and learning, my

unselfish
        maneuverings

as I'd slide her
over myself, at just the right speed,

the right pressure,
like an eraser.

## Cozy Restaurant

Its flame nearly frozen, protected
by a glass fitting,

this ruby candle
stands with great

prescience.   Mouth and tongue rule
in my cloister

of appetite. Here is a realm for memories,
a certain disposition. Decades

of good times
framed by rooms—the alcohol

and smoky fog, the heaven
of intimacy, the tastes

between legs—
are floating around this place. I'm drunk

in the red decor
and in the silence I invent. Who could guess

that middle age, well-fed and tired,
could call this up, now,

with wife and two
yapping children, at this table? They

are here, but I am far away
in many places. Beer

and more beer. I can't
get enough—I'm a smile dumb

as a baby staring
at a red balloon.   That flame's a crystal ball

or maybe a cocoon. If I look closely
I can see it!—the old smoke

hosting the ghosts, in miniature,
on the tabletop,

my world of joys and freedom
gathering strength

like a batch of toys
tossed from a chest, pleasing a child.

## Encounter

He strolls triumphant
in the early light

while she sleeps. Aren't these
Palladian windows? He stares as a god might

at the garden below,
thinking of the wild dream that woke him—

of roads and running,
gangsters in black suits,
                          hats with no heads,

crazy. But it's festival time
near Elkhorn, Nebraska,

and hot air balloons, gaudy and grand
upwind, upwest,
                      surprise him briefly

way out there on the plains.
They mark the horizon, they rise and

approach him
slowly, with deference.
                        *This is right,*

he thinks,    and lifts his head
toward the new blue, hair reaching

down his back,
while she watches him,
>	one eye open
>	above the damp pillow.

# At the Artist Retreat

*a word from Blake*

A man walks between historic buildings
followed by cartoon clouds
of attacking mosquitoes
buzzing like tinnitus,
a bad ear.
    But look! Up there, the future
watching, the admiring
blue. A few clouds are leaning
at this moment
in the direction of
his unspoken wit.
   ~

    In his room, a window
captures it best : joy-filled certainty
holds a page two feet in front of his eyes
and fills the frame with what he calls
*immensity.*
   ~

   The bell rings
announcing dinner. Relationships
are tricky, aren't they. There's literature
and these tables — and who'll be sitting with us.

# Fallen

*an evening party in August*

It's hard finding a summit here, an outpost
where his colors might fly:

the screen door opening
to announce the famous author

is a Fugito Scale event
to gnats on the mesh.   The man inside

is feeling outside, has trouble performing
when *the great one*

cracks a joke.
General laughter is a cold wind on his body,

so he tries to stay warm
and laughs a little too loud.

He doesn't have much left.
With nods and soft hands, he musters,

he blusters,   one last show
before he goes, coursing through hierarchy,

the shadow-lit contours
of necks and arms and breasts,

the shifting patterns of light on glasses of wine.
Outside—finally!—

he walks sideways from the door,
saying goodbye    to the faces turning away.

# Teaching

*her death*

The book-covered wall
does not block his vision.

Behind it, no pages, no
"Vigil Strange"

near alphabet's end—
just the long tunnel. If I grab a book

and point out Heathcliff
living each day

living at the end—no.
There's only himself

and the old business
that gets harder each time

—this time
he will not transform the pain

into the good bitterness
of a very pure chocolate.

He'll draw back his sight,
collecting the emptiness,

and see the books again,
their respectful postures,

how they shout their names
when called upon.

He'll whisper
a few thoughts to them

while he reads—
and brush his fingers over the lines.

## Collector

*a nod to Lars Gustafsson*

His glasses bear down
on children's books, first editions

with prized illustrations in color. What pleasure,
touching the edges

of those pages, smell of old paper
on fingertips—oh the air

will take him
where he needs to go. Arthur's blue stockings

are louder than any call
from outside the walls. The sword

comes out like a splinter.     Clamped together
by two red moons on its fuselage,

a tiny Japanese *Zero*
is ready to fly from the mantle.

His mother asks about work
and puts the tray of food on his lap.

She can see that he's flying hard, this warrior
with so many lives on his mind.

The old patients at the VA
enjoy his talk

while he guides them down the hall,
his unhurried way of listening

to their histories and gripes, this man
who places their lungs,

their bones, against the x-ray plates.
He'll see them in battle tonight.

## Modestly Alive

He'd found it himself,
the tiny gland in his neck—the doctor, impressed,

calmed him
with examples of lively imagination.

>*Nothing*, she said,
>*it hasn't been growing*—

meaning: such fear
would find no soon retreat,

and she was right: eighteen years
since that day, fast ones, a scoop of dirt

thrown from a shovel. The gamesmanship
of anxiety

collapses time,
though humor flares from that cloister

on occasion, with strange potentials,
a speculative

world, for instance, where his genetic markers
could be shaped

into a bold-face "O"
in a supercomputer at MIT. Oh, he'd last till the sun

goes out, through conversions of data, upgrades
of technology,

modestly alive, philosophers would posit,
in complexity enough

to be a primitive
sentient form.
    That would do

except reality
imposes:

   At today's lecture

we'll look at truth in abundance—telomeres
dangling from cell walls.

~


His daughter crawls on a glass grid
at the university Infant Lab,

dumbly mapping
randomness and space, smiling in bright light—

   but it's her night terrors that concern him.
   Aren't they actually

numbers of a sort—chaos, a lack
of order?

    Telomeres get shorter

with age, their heads
bunching like stubble

or stiff wires cracking
the walls of old cells—

                        mutations are well-fed babies
                        frolicking in the entropy.

Sometimes his hand counts time on the kitchen table:

the clicking wedding ring
is the voice.

# A Room for Last Rites

*a fantasia*


... catching everything lost from the blood,
supernatural, red
with oxygen,
        glowing,
                Matisse.    No windows, not even
Emily Dickinson's blue. No leaving
whatsoever : dad, cat, self, what-
ever.      I want the walls angled inwards
to protect the soul, as with Beckman, whose in-
lighted colors
compress time and
                cage it. I will be a baby again
or else the adult thing : a hopeless person
who won't face it.
               Wallpaper might work, endless
repetitions    of windmills, or    old Chinese peasants
pulling carts to some-where
over and over : benedictions
                   always mid-speech —
fractals, repeating,
going out from the frame,    into faith
and the start    of whatever happened last.

## Above It, Below It

*grass-green carpet*

This home is a strange child who keeps its mouth shut —
grown old,     finding expression
in shag carpet threads
one brother collected in a bag
to paste back down when needed,
money scarce.     I bounce the bag in my hands
and we can't stop laughing.
                    Around us, dirt
on the walls, shit paint, a toggle switch
for lights that don't work, and a TV
turned up loud.

~

            Subterranean hurt, a form
of love tunneling. Would it be too painful to confront our deficits
and make ourselves vulnerable?
                    *Yes.*
                        One lives with a wink,
a tic. Yet we don't want to go on like servants,
do we?
        A thirsty rat has drowned
            in the pail of water you drew last night from the creek.
I want to hear the sound of our voices and not our voices
speaking through filters. I want to clean the windows finally
— feel sunlight to the point of burning.

## Wavelengths

1.
Damp white sheets
hanging on lines

are brushing over his mind, cooling his face
even now
        —he's running through them a long time ago.

It's late summer surely. Cicadas call
to where the end might be.

           ~

           Silver dollars
           you rolled on the hardwood

floor of *the old house*
go a lengthy passage

you can hardly measure. You hear them
trailing away
        redshifting, falling,

jangling to a stop.

           ~

        You're the training halfback

dragging a parachute
behind yourself, as fast as you can. You hate it.

*I'd rather stumble curious*
*through seconds*

*and each day be —*
*not this thing, not this — but a day.*


2.
It's hard taking a walk
without running into yourself — what happened

to surprise?
        The muscled water snake with dark diamonds
        I saw beside the pond today

amazes for the time
a signal
        crosses a hub
        of neurons in the brain — then

childhood again, the time I saw
the same snake

caught with stick and sure hands

— this hologram
        I want to escape.


3.
On TV: *The Daytona 500*. He enjoys
the sharp
        stripping sound

of pit crews tearing off
film after film
               on windshields

as each gets dirty. When a wreck
carries the leader

across the finish line—it's pure,
clean.
            He jumps from the chair screaming.

# EMERSON

> *If a story or a poem of mine is successful,*
> *its success springs from a deeper source...*
> —BORGES

Your neighbor hands you an ax
and grips
         the eaten-out fence.

*Look at these bugs,* he says,
but your mind is on

the oil spill
in the Gulf, the Company
                  and State—*What?*

*These bugs. They eat the rot and make it worse.*
*Look.*
      You barely hear and say

*Oh, yes.* He wants to know if you're positive
you want to work
              this heavy ax—

you can grab a hammer
later, if you want,
              and help him pound nails.

*No no, of course not.*
*Let's get going*
            —and after a few swings

muscles bring you home.

You can't believe your strength, your
pleasure,
          as you smash the boards down.

You stop for a moment
and pick one up,
          looking for a crevice,

the darkness and stinking rot, the bugs
inches below your eye.

## The Healthy

Those who don't dwell
have a way about them. They're funny    and walk like wings

into the winds. *Dwell* means clay in the brain,
the past changing shapes with too much thinking—

to get it right. At fever-house
the weathervane is rusted into place

but the chimney sways in a dream—
                          all those heat waves
                          and drifting smoke.

Hailed by the hand    stuck waving from optimism,
the healthy jut their chins into circumstance—persistent

punch-drunk fighters who can't say *enough*, who don't hear
the bell. They keep going    all the way to *repeat*

on the boom box—
                they throw their memories into the feast
                after the funeral

when a liquored relation breaks a glass while dancing.
Isn't he funny! Isn't he the road    back to work.

# III

*I'd sooner, except the penalties, kill a man than a hawk...*

—Robinson Jeffers

## Redwoods: Northern California

*4% left*

Decay     gets woven into branches, dust
and bits of bark,

dried grasses
blown up     over two centuries

to a height where soil shouldn't be —
where needles cluster,     a fractal

plane higher
than Amazon canopy,
     alien enough, far enough
     from waking voices

to be the dream     where fairy tales find wings before
coming down.

~

These trees hold up,     they control
movement of water in a parallel earth:

soil and ponds
in scaled-back versions of what we know —

fissure rivers     no bigger than crayon marks
from a child, driven
by slow drips,
    take their time in the rain.

Announcement : This brain is higher,     and more fine-tuned
because of the wind
blowing through arms on either side.

~

With so much seeding from wind
this place hangs on, protected

for now, the noise of earth movers
still unheard, despite
                a thickening ring
                of scar tissue.

~

Here is the floating earth where I've always lived anyway,

        the height between
        cloud and calling—

. . . and more than one kind of place can house a person.

This tree, for instance, swayed by wind
and sheer momentum

reveals its name if it had one:

*the texture of height in relation to ground*
*as brokered by wind*:
                a lab-tag for bloodwork.

~

Above me—smell of burning.

Lights blink off and on
behind a door of fog
                built from heat and wet air.

                It's a dream chamber,
                the slow glow

of a mind at work: Taller than I, a fire cave
smolders
where lightning hit the massive trunk,

but redwoods don't care if they burn,    they use the burn

and take their time
in the high air
            building stories in the holes.

## Ghost Bat

*Belize, 1999*

We don't sleep on Temash River
but scan searchlights

defined by insects and mist,
dropping our eyes now and again

to check the screen
for the 22-kilohertz call

of the Ghost Bat. Unmoving
with focus, his face

swollen from *doctor flies*
biting through repellant, Colin watches

the artificial sky,
looking for white wings. I bait a fly rod

with a sphinx moth
and wave it high

while he points the light
—and we fish in the air,

knowing how to hook the bat
by wing unhurt

and bring it to science
to keep it alive

beyond the look of things here,
all the destruction.

How silly we must appear
in the lighted night, pole in air,

to anyone watching
our drifting down the slow river.

## Bull Snake

*Sherburne Refuge, Minnesota*

Twisted, dead-muscled,
killed by a driver

careless or wanting
to kill—
        the sand-colored snake

thick as a bat
on blacktop of County Road 9

is cracking apart,
its crosshatched head

brittle and flat:
        a graph, a
        "business as usual."

It wanted a slope
a few steps from here—leading to grasses,

to rocks and low shrubs
of savanna, networks of rodents.

      *Heat waves loosen*
      *boulders moving*
      *as though alive in the distance. . . .*

    No car but my own

in sight
at this moment—*this one,*

                *and there is no distance—*

and bright sun
adds a hyper note

to the anxiety diffusing my anger.
The scales in my grip

feel perverse, their sharp edges
ready for movement

                *—but the dirty,*
                *dried blood*
                *near my fingers.*

I throw it far as I can
where it wanted to go.

## The Parrot Left Behind

> *an adult African Grey possesses the intelligence of a young toddler—plus a store of memories and practical wisdom*

1.
The Grey came back in a dream. I didn't know the story—
the black bark around him

and a shine inside the internal distance
suggested intent,

a discomfort
with someone's judgment, but he didn't have me to blame.

Wings unclipped, he'd flown away
before we moved.
                      My mom said I climbed stacks of boxes
                      looking, calling....

*Gone for good,*
she said then—
                  *like cats* bothered by ragged nerves, upheaval

in rooms. But she knew where he was:
the edge of hanging mosses, the cypress woods

a short walk behind the house.
She didn't want the trouble. *At that age you'd forget.*

2.
I knew its lifespan,
Its deep knowledge of preferred range—and drove a long day

in hot sun,
        the windshield a lens on my body. White letters
        glared on green

highway signs announcing distance. The right angles
of lettering—strange,

disturbing. One might feel unalive in machinery this bright.

Flat maps, flat time, with algorithms
of chance—otherworldly,

        this cold
        presentation, maybe unsolvable.

3.
The property, still vast,
held blue sky
        on the tips of its trees—too close,

this sky, too compressed and out of time. An older man
answering the door,
        the second owner since my parents,

said ok to walking the place, amused
with questions about a parrot. *A Grey's been here*

*I don't know how long. We get all kinds—escapees.*
*Some stay for years.*
        He said it talked a lot, sounds / words

that could be anything, where trees begin out back.

4.
The bird's in tangles of a large cypress, low
and shaded from sun.
                      Continuity
                      is the look of things here,

and belief has few requirements. "You Dirty Boy?
Come on, bring it back." I mention old family

and repeat my dad's name *Bill*
to see what the bird might find
                              inside that syllable.

Something would remain. Any smart creature
can be impacted
                    by touch, by insistent
                    tones of speech

that help form a brain. If this is him,
I wonder what's happened
                            to what he said years ago.

5.
In the dream, I yelled at my mom,
knowing her guilt: leaving this animal behind —

and now maybe its news.

She said he was happier
free outside, in the endless summer of trees in Houston.

6.
I watch myself talking
in disbelief: *Sorry*, I say—*Did you miss*

*my yelling and running?* Words give peace,
room to imagine
                a filled vagueness. How much

can he recall? I'd like to know life then. A few details
would be something—

                but I most want words
                about family who've died—alive,

healthy at that time. *It still hurts*
the dream said—
                and that's what I take away. The Grey

speaks a rapid language—some of it words
maybe just in my mind.
                I'm edging closer now,

wanting to stroke the nape,
                but crown feathers rise
                and the wings get ready.

## A Chinese Mantis

Soon to die,
it sheds for the last time—

and wings!—
here they are at last, drying off

for delivery
of an egg case, a few clumsy flights

before the first frost. Maybe it won't
choose to leave

this dense box-plant
beside the house

where it's been a friend
since May, when a dozen, newly hatched,

encircled my ring. It jumps toward me
when I spray water

to find it—camouflaged
ready to kill—but seems to enjoy crawling

over my palm and fingers
with its devilish

and constant smile. Like a hosta leaf
in the wind's minor third—

or else an arrogant champion
promising a knockout—

the head moves side to side, that ironic
heart-shaped head

channeling the brain
into the smiling, dead-set mouth.

# Hooded Warbler

*an ars poetica, migration*

I can't fix on
the song diffracted by leaves,

the nervous, the still
growing,
        leaves of the forest

anxious to control
the space here.
            The song in flight

washes the compass
while the song
        at rest
        on a branch

builds a top hat
into which
        one might throw a little money

if one could. I see the source
in my mind, but that's not enough:

color's my shelter
—a warm bar    an escort of jets—

and the color of song is a species of bird
at rest or in flight.

The leaves of nesting time work me too hard,

but how can one be disappointed
when mystery wins,
                          the bird unseen,

and spirit fills
so much brilliant space.

## To the Brown Recluse

*rarely, a bite leads to amputation*

Skilled beyond the teeth
of deadly solutions,

of white powders puffed into cracks by experts,
you alone

escape the guarantees of
*companies,*   having learned where the ghosts are

and their subtlety.
But no divining rods will ever cross

to pinpoint your long-legged poise.   The vents are yours,
light fixtures, the dark

worlds behind drywall—still, because of my glue traps
and toggle switches I snap

on the nights you relish, your numbers are down to *occult,*
like cancer cells hiding, biding

their time—your clan, still
persisting, even as a hand-held shoe

knocks you dead on the carpet. I've pictured the voids
you inhabit   and know the limits of action

and've heard for too long
the violin you lug around on your back. Its minor key

sounds like an ice pick,
the cold stabbings of killers. I'm certain

your tiny shed skins    that line the chimney
fly up from the fire like kites.

# IV

*And the fierce thunders roar me their music*
*And the winds shriek through the clouds mad, opposing,*
*And through all the riven skies God's swords clash.*

—Ezra Pound

# This Place Is Mine

My friend Jack, who doesn't much worry about death,
sent me a poem called "Thief"

by Jean Follain. On the right edge of the copy, Jack's palm print
interrupts the black strip

of what seems like a starless night
behind the poem. He's pushing the book hard:

the dark line between pages — thin
with insistence,     desire for clarity.

It's hard to read this poem with so much pressure behind it.
Jack's fingers must be bent

at the first knuckles and turning red
against the spine.   The poem features a thief,

a man stealing milk from a cow in broad daylight,
under what Follain calls a timeless sun.

Maybe that's why the guy, sated,
falls asleep on the grass. We never learn his technique,

which is just as well. I feel the burden of Jack pushing
all this world at me,

the happy sleep of the thief
under blue sky.   The empty night weighs nothing,

stretching out like a hallway behind the poem, going on
forever perhaps, with its own brand

of possibilities. This place is mine more than Jack's—
except for his palm print, its upbeat

chatter   like a distant radio,
while I take a walk here, sliding my fingers along the wall.

# My Dolls

The person must be dead.
When courage is demanded

I open my attaché case. I pull out a doll
from my collection,

a likeness
of someone from my past, a dead one

I loved
who gives me strength

in tune
with the situation. The person must be dead

because only in death
does magic work.

I carry my dolls with conviction.
I grip one tight and stare at the face—then

act: dot dot dot. Above me:

the hovering cloud of death.
My case is black, and I'm the agent

named Go To Hell.
I direct a secret code around myself

like a tornado. Everyone gets hurt.
I'm left—in glory—alone.

# HOMAGE TO SERGIO LEONE

*(for Ennio Morricone)*

*Such films as* Once Upon a Time in the West *and* For a Few Dollars More *from Italian director Sergio Leone created a new myth of the American west that focused on complex but driven individuals.*


    The sharp
    edge. . . the shadow line

    of a black hat    solves the blue eyes
    it cuts across.

    A single
    face

    fills the screen,
    Fonda poised against

    Bronson, whose own face, its rugged
    hachured map,

    takes its turn
    before us. "Once upon a time"

    dry gulches
    ran blue—but for now

    they won't. For now    Community
    (small

as philosophy)
is a lie.

Who could even think it?
"Something

to do with death"    primes the hot air,
the blue sky, that sun—

it's in the calm
positioning of their bodies

ready to snap
in outright contention—it powers

who they are    and the pain
they execute.

## "Smooth Bore, Scattergun"

> *you are*
> *the only one*
> *to cover me*
> *when I sleep, cover me*
> *in my dreams...*
> —The Ramones, "Scattergun"

> ...*it is but lost time to converse*
> *with you whose works are only Analytics.*
> —William Blake, The Marriage of Heaven and Hell

Violence is calming,     available
to set things right

in the mind — unreal
but it works. The reach

of what must be done
is a bridge, and fog pushing in mustn't

win the day. Denial's
an easy abdication — if it wins the soul,

one is a fruit slit open
to the circling red wasps

of late summer.     There's a complex of
passive-aggressiveness

factoried and laminated
in various cultural centers:    it's in-

comprehensible
but no different from a toad's tongue

snapping up the bug. That words
do more damage

than fist to jaw—a lie, a
protocol. But nothing said or done

comes close in force
to fantasies of torque, of glaring

dirt-driven hands:    the calming violence,
the specificity

and brilliant invulnerability:    the lotion
in the tightly folded brain.

## His Secret

The great power-forward    knew one way to play:
drive to the basket, explode

to the rim, his two arms
forming a diamond—
                his faith:
                no one could stop him,

no two—
        he attacked with his shoulder

splitting them, fighting through
with both hands
                vice-gripping the ball—one dribble

and up with both elbows
                *to keep the space pure.*

Not Thurmond or Reed, not Chamberlain,
not even Russell could stop him

forty-eight minutes. His game—brutal,
nose broken
            six times, cartilage

like clay. A cheap foul took his knee for a year.
Teammates loved him.
                        His revenge:
                        *scoreboard—*

a nature that digs into loss and won't take it,

and one loss
              he never talked about, nothing
              to do with ball,

. . . broke him apart
              *—so many gaps*
              *to bring home—*

a long time ago    not long for him
that kept him moving,

pounding—
        *. . . tension*
        *spreading over his skin,    a total*
        *focus,*

              *as though listening*
              *to a whisper*
                    *in the deafening arena.*

# The Neighbor's Truck

Nearly falling, raising my foot
chest level
to the steel step,
              I pulled myself

into the huge
high cab, its leather seat
              black, ripped,
              scraping my bare thighs—

the energy around me    pressed on my head
like a giant shell
            held to the ear.

He threw branches into the bed with thundering bangs.

        "Let's go!"

and we banged along the rutted road, the wheels
spinning monsters,

thick limbs hammering behind me,   laughter
to my left

           —no seat belts on this wild flight—

my parents, their white sedan,
getting farther away.

Dozens of little brick homes, alert to our activity,

curved around us
on the flat land
            as we drove past the corn rows,

that one remaining field,
                and disappeared
                into the woods.

# Italian Cook

*at the island retreat*

With angles and momentum,
his Roman nose

amplifies
the mighty force below it:

> his gut — stuffed
> with happy negligence,

> pulling him forward
> tilting him backward

> at the same time —
> projecting, one might say,

command, or *(at the least)* unbudgable
balance.
         Giorgio is the kitchen.

He talks English like lobster claws
clicking above his grip.

He spits rocks from his mouth. Once only
one of us touched a knob

in his kitchen
(a little knob, leading to cereal bowls):

we learned about transitions,
we saw his finger

shake with violence    in front of
his screaming
                mouth—*Leave me alone!*

*Leave me alone!* We stepped outside
the open door,
                guilty, perplexed, punished
                in the shining fog.

# Selective

*the Old Masters*

I lift my head, I lift the can
and pour it down,

toasting the ancients
in the ceiling
        *—the nearest sky—*

my people
akin to English
        soccer hooligans

or fat guys with chips, who cheer the tv
and slap the backs

of ecstatic dogs,
        ancients

who blathered and drooled over tables
cracked
        with daggers striking

in support
of the night's truth.
            I see you looking
            down, shaking

your scarred and bearded faces,
spitting out my faults

with sneers and curses, with horrible laughter
I want to join.

## Late Afternoon at Kolac's the Sun is Remade

*Prague, NE*

Drink tall beer and spill it
dripping from your chin, shining

on polyester—
and dump sugar into the coffee. Glare

on the window is band-light,
and notes kicked up from the dirt street

are the gold tuba's
brontosaurian reach. Three fat old guys

making music, those
unremarkable shades of grey

who'd been hiding under their skins,
are blue shale now,

ageless with fossils. Irony
is bad taste.

Like *magic bullets*
for a disease that used to be terminal,

balls of sun
hail from the accordion, a purity post

post-modern, plain
beyond. Where! Where have they gone,

our tedium and pain. The dumb drums
frame the saving.

## Happy Tongue

*When we learnt the use of the phrase 'so-and-so has a toothache' we were pointed out certain kinds of behavior of those who were said to have toothache. As an instance... let us take holding your cheek.*
—WITTGENSTEIN, *The Blue Book*

*Now should we say that B on seeing the pencil after seeing instruments he didn't know had a feeling of familiarity? ... He saw a pencil, smiled, felt relieved, and the name of the object he saw came into his mind or mouth.*
—WITTGENSTEIN, *The Brown Book*

    What chambered nautilus
    on my shelf of oddities

    gave birth to the crimson pigeon
    cruising a level plane

    outside my window?    Curled around
    my jar of pencils

    Jack shot me a glance
    and cleaned his paws with a happy tongue.

    I took my car to the shop and shook
    the mechanic's hand.

    His nose suggested a drinker
    and when he sneezed the day

    retreated with me.               But I got home

secured with shining
new tires, new timing belt,

and then by god nothing out back
but the tomatoes

—big beautiful bloods—
my window properly filtered.

# The Windmill Machine

*off the grid*

Lightning struck it
and burnt the circuit dead. Soon the wind

driving it
stopped
  and birdsong, too,
   in needles of spruce:

stillness, like white-feathered seeds
stuck on a window screen.

The truth came clear under the settled dust:
I'm a passenger

in a big machine, the windmill
an engine,
   nature
   an alien thing. Such a weird universe.

If the captain brings his boat to this island,
I'll go back to the mainland

but what will it be that I'm crossing
and what trick awaits me on the journey back?

The windmill exists
between the pulses

>            we feel in our necks.
>            It used to answer

the questions we've wondered about. Fixing it
is our lives.

## Killing Art

*11,000 BCE, the Clovis People*

In their minds
picturing
        ideal facets and deadly lines,

they knapped phosphoria
—a rare and brilliant killer—

holding it up to the sky
to gauge the precision

to penetrate mammoth,
their fingers
        bloodied by edges
        that cut with a touch.

Other good killing machines

were drawn from the earth at this time
—agate, jasper, opal—

and shaped into more
than practical art.
        Knowing the dangers
        of facing the beast,

their pleasure was deep
tying point to shaft:
        symmetry of handwork,

luminous rock and its power to kill—
they did it to live.

                       Like crumpled pages,
                       spalls lie in heaps

in the courts where they worked,
but the final lights
                       tore into flesh.